BUTTERCREAM BOOK:

A Collection of The Best Recipes

MARIA SOBININA

m-a-i-a.com & maiatea.com

MARIA SOBININA   m-a-i-a.com

Copyright © 2019 - 2021 MARIA SOBININA
m-a-i-a.com & maiatea.com

All rights reserved.

ISBN-13: 9781792789434

DEDICATION

This book is dedicated to my beautiful family and friends, as well as to you, my reader. I am happy to share the amazing joy of preparing healthy meals with you.

At m-a-i-a.com and MaiaTea.com we give back to the community. Every week we feed more than 100 people in need and provide them with the basic essentials. Sign up for our FREE recipes and stay tuned for our updates. cookbooks@m-a-i-a.com with Recipes in the subject.

MAIA

TABLE OF CONTENTS

What is Buttercream?   6

Buttercream Ingredients   7

Professional Buttercream   10

Flavoured Buttercream   10

Buttercream Types   12

Equipment for Making Buttercream   15

Buttercream Tips   18

Recipes: Base Buttercream   20

American Buttercream   20

Swiss Meringue Buttercream   22

German Buttercream   24

Vanilla Cream Buttercream   27

French Buttercream   29

Italian Meringue Buttercream   31

Buttercream for Flower Piping   34

Cream Cheese Buttercream   36

Recipes: Fondant & Icing   38

Rolled Fondant *(Sculpting)*   38

Rolled Fondant *(Gum Paste)*   40

Poured Fondant   42

Marzipan Icing   43

Royal Icing   45

Chocolate Ganache   46

Quick and Simple Buttercream   48

Recipes: Flavoured Buttercream   50

German Chocolate Buttercream   50

Almond Buttercream   52

Banana Buttercream   54

Paradise Island Buttercream   56

Caramel Dreams Buttercream   58

Go Nuts Cream Cheese Buttercream   60

Hazelnut Buttercream   62

Cream Cheese Dream Buttercream   64

Lemon Cream Cheese Buttercream   66

Chocolate Marshmallow Fondant   68

Snow White Buttercream   70

Christmas Eggnog Buttercream   72

Raspberry Buttercream   74

Black Volcano Buttercream   76

Morning Joy Coffee Buttercream   78

Amaretto-Maple Cream Cheese Buttercream   80

Avocado Buttercream   82

Champagne Buttercream   84

White Chocolate Buttercream   86

Strawberry Cream Cheese Frosting   88

Dark Chocolate Buttercream   90

White Chocolate Glaze   92

Vanilla Buttercream   94

Amaretto Buttercream   96

Marshmallow Fluff Buttercream   98

Silver Mountain Buttercream   100

Peanut Butter Buttercream   102

Caramel Buttercream   104

Blueberry Buttercream   106

Dark Horse Chocolate Cream Cheese Buttercream   109

Almond Vanilla Icing   111

Banana Buttercream   112

Banana Cream Cheese Buttercream   114

Banana Caramel Buttercream   116

Strawberry Glaze   118

Unbaked Meringue Icing   120

Cinnamon Glaze   122

Pineapple Coconut Buttercream   124

Maple Meringue Icing   126

Marshmallow Buttercream   128

Caramel Buttercream   130

Vegan Peanut Buttercream   132

White-Dark Chocolate Buttercream   134

Maple Buttercream   136

Chocolate Buttercream   138

Cherry Buttercream   140

White Russian Buttercream   143

Rum Raisin Cream Buttercream   145

Red Wine Cream Buttercream   148

What is Buttercream?

Buttercream, as the name indicates, is made of butter, as the main ingredient. It is important to use a good-quality butter to ensure the buttercream is tasty. Select the butter that tastes good and has high-fat content. Make sure your butter is unsalted, or your buttercream may have a salty taste.

Buttercream is used to decorate tops and sides of cakes and cupcakes, and as a filling between the cake's layers.

There are different basic recipes of buttercream. Some recipes call for using only butter, while others call for adding vegetable shortening, or heavy cream, to name a few.

Adding vegetable shortening makes buttercream more stable and easier to use for piping flowers. It also makes it more heat-proof. However, the taste of all-butter buttercream is superior, as buttercream with vegetable shortening may have a less pleasing taste.

When you add cream cheese or heavy cream in your buttercream, you should refrigerate the buttercream. This buttercream is not optimal to use for piping complex flowers or decorations. You can still pipe swirls on cakes and cupcakes.

Buttercream Ingredients

Butter

Buttercream recipes call for softened butter. What does this mean? Softened butter should keep shape when pressed down by a finger. Typically, depending on the temperature in your kitchen, it takes between thirty minutes to an hour to soften the butter. You can speed up the process by unwrapping and cutting the butter on pieces.

Sugar

Depending on a recipe, you will use either *powdered sugar* or *granulated sugar*. Granulated sugar is used in meringue-based buttercream recipes. These recipes require heating, and granulated sugar melts well when it is heated.

Powdered sugar is used in recipes that do not contain eggs. Powdered sugar is easier to mix with butter to create a smooth consistency.

It is recommended to sift powdered sugar prior to mixing it with butter. This will prevent creating lumps in your buttercream.

Do not use granulated sugar in non-meringue buttercream because you will feel sugar granules in the recipe.

It is best to use cane sugar (not beet sugar) to create the best texture and quality of buttercream.

Eggs

Some buttercream recipes call for using eggs when others do not require eggs. Meringue-based buttercreams make it easier to pipe complex shapes.

There is a way, however, to make eggless buttercream more stable and acceptable for piping. When you add cornstarch or corn flour, your buttercream becomes more stable.

Make sure to use organic corn starch and corn flour as corn products are likely to be genetically manipulated (GMO).

If you are afraid to use raw eggs, you can pasteurize eggs before using them in your recipe. To pasteurize eggs, place a waterproof bowl into a saucepan and add water to cover half of the bowl height.

Then place eggs into the bowl and heat the water up to 140°F. Let it boil for three minutes to heat up the eggs. Do not let the water heat over 142°F.

Milk & Heavy Cream

When you are adding milk to buttercream, make sure it is whole milk. Whole milk contains more fat. Alliteratively, you can add heavy cream.

Vanilla Extract

Vanilla enhances flavors. For instance, if the recipe uses chocolate, coffee, or fruit syrups, adding vanilla enhances the flavor of additives.

Vanilla extract comes in natural and artificial forms. A natural vanilla extract is superior to artificial vanilla extract. To create the best quality buttercream, use natural vanilla extract.

Almond Extract

The basic buttercream recipe does not call for using almond extract. Almond extract, however, enhances the taste.

The pure almond extract includes three primary ingredients: alcohol, water, and almond oil. To create the best quality buttercream and to add additional richness to your buttercream use natural almond extract.

Professional Buttercream

Professional buttercream utilizes simple ingredients, such as butter, eggs (for meringue-based buttercreams), sugar, milk or heavy cream, vanilla extract, and, in some instances, corn flour.

Flavoured Buttercream

You can use flavored buttercream for the recipes you make for your friends and family. Addition of flavors may make this buttercream less stable.

You can make your buttercream taste more interesting by introducing flavors and colors to the base recipe.

Ready to Use Flavors:

You can create your own flavors, or you can use existing flavors such as coffee, Irish cream, and Vanilla.

You can make your flavors from berries, fruits, chocolate and more.

Fruit & Berries Flavors

To make flavors from fruits, make fruit syrup by adding sugar to fresh or frozen fruits. Then reduce the liquid by heating the mixture and simmering it on low heat until it reaches the desired consistency. Reduce most of the liquids to avoid making runny buttercream.

Chocolate Flavors:

For chocolate buttercream select dark, regular or white baker's chocolate. Heat the chocolate over a water bath on low heat until chocolate melts.

Nut Flavors:

You can add nut butter, such as almond butter, or you can add nut spreads like chocolate Nutella spread.

Marshmallow Fluff

When you add marshmallow fluff, your buttercream will hold the shape when swirled on top of cakes and cupcakes. You can also use it as a filling between the layers of your cakes. This buttercream tends to be more for at-home use.

Sugar Glue is used to attached fondant decorations to the cake. Add a small amount of water to a piece of fondant. Set aside for a few minutes. Stir before using.

Buttercream Types

There are many types of buttercream, but most popular kinds are American Buttercream, Swiss Meringue, Italian Meringue, and French buttercreams.

American Buttercream

American Buttercream is a combination of butter and powdered sugar, in one to two proportion. This buttercream is easy to make. This is a great base buttercream for adding flavors.

This buttercream is best for designs that require firmer icing. American buttercream is not ideal for piping flowers.

Swiss Meringue Buttercream

Swiss Meringue Buttercream is made by heating egg whites and sugar and mixing until sugar dissolves. Then the mixture is whipped into a meringue. And lastly, softened butter is added to the mixture.

Swiss Meringue Buttercream is ideal for cake exteriors, piping flowers, and icing cakes and cupcakes.

Italian Meringue Buttercream

Italian Meringue Buttercream is made by heating *water* and *sugar*, constantly mixing until sugar dissolves. Then the mixture is added to egg whites and whipped into a meringue. And finely, softened butter is added to the mixture.

Italian Meringue Buttercream is ideal for cake exteriors, piping flowers, and icing cakes and cupcakes.

French Buttercream

French Buttercream is made by heating *water* and *sugar*, and mixing until sugar dissolves. Then the mixture is added to egg yolks. And lastly, softened butter is added to the mixture.

French Buttercream is ideal for cake exteriors, piping flowers, and icing cakes and cupcakes.

Rolled Fondant

Rolled fondant does not have butter, and it is technically not a buttercream. Rolled fondant is a pliable sugar dough rolled into thin sheets. Rolled fondant is used to wrap around a cake to create colorful and even surfaces.

The main ingredients in rolled fondant are glucose syrup, glycerin, powdered sugar, and gelatin.

Rolled fondant is a vital component in cake decorations. It is utilized to wrap cakes as well as to make fondant decorations.

Rolled fondant can be used as **sculpting fondant** or as **sugar paste** (*or gum paste*). Sculpting fondant is more stiff and stretchy, whereas sugar paste is firm when hardens. Sculpting fondant is used to cover cakes. Sugar paste is utilized to make decorations.

Poured Fondant

Unlike rolled fondant, poured fondant is a soft icing used to drizzle over cakes, cupcakes, cookies or pastries. You can also fill this icing in candies.

Marzipan Icing

Marzipan icing has a smooth, flat finish and an exquisite nut flavor. It can be utilized instead of rolled fondant to create decorations. Marzipan icing has a clay-like consistency.

Marzipan icing, a popular sugar paste, contains more natural ingredients and fewer chemicals than rolled fondant.

Equipment for Making Buttercream

Basic equipment for buttercream project:

- **Stand mixer** or **hand mixer** equipped with a paddle attachment. Stand mixers are typically more powerful than a hand mixer.

- A **Silicone spatula** is used to scrape the sides and the bottom of your mixing bowl.

- A **Sifter** is useful to sift powdered sugar and salt to avoid lumps in the buttercream.

- **Medium saucepan** and **heat-proof bowl** to create a water bath to incorporate and pasteurize eggs as well as to make sugar and fruit syrups.

- A **Food Processor** is used to process fruit and sugar mixture into fruit syrups. You can also use it to make nut butter.

- **Turn Table** makes it easier to decorate cakes and create a smooth and even finishing on the sides of the cake.

- **Leveling Spatula** helps to create an even finishing on the sides and the top of the cake.

- With a **Rolling Pin,** you will roll fondants into a thin wrap-like layer to wrap around the cake.

- Once you cover the cake with a rolled fondant, use **Fondant Smoother** to make the cake's surface more even and to release air bubbles.

- **Paint Brushes** are essential to add a small amount of water or sugar glue to attach fondant decorations.

- **Sharp Knife / X-Acto Blade** is helpful to cut rolled fondant. This equipment is essential to create rolled fondant decorations as well as to create an even cut surfaces when wrapping your cake with rolled fondant.

- **Piping Tips** are used to pipe buttercream to create shapes, swirls, and flowers. There is a wide variety of piping tips shapes.

- A **coupler** is a plastic ring used to attach piping tips to a piping bag. A coupler makes it possible to interchange piping tips without exchanging the piping bag filled with buttercream.

- **Piping Bags.** Piping bags made of silicone are durable and reusable. Piping bags made of transparent plastic bag material are one-time use bags.

Buttercream Tips

Tip 1: Do not overbeat your buttercream. If you are beating your butter without any additives, you can beat it as long as you desire. Some kinds of butter are pale, other kinds of butter are more yellow in color.

Typically, you will beat the butter for one to two minutes, but If you want to achieve a lighter buttercream color, beat butter for a longer time.

Tip 2: Once you added any other ingredients to the butter, **limit beating to 20 to 30 seconds** or less.

Tip 3: **Sift powdered sugar** at least once. This will prevent the creation of lumps, and your buttercream will be smoother.

Tip 4: When you are beating buttercream, make sure you periodically **scrape the sides of the bowl and mixer blades** to incorporate and evenly mix all ingredients.

Tip 5: If a recipe requires raw eggs, you can pasteurize eggs by placing eggs into a cold water bath, heating water to 138°F and simmering eggs for four minutes.

Tip 6: Use **cane sugar** versus beet sugar to create a

smoother consistency buttercream.

Tip 7: If your buttercream is too stiff **add water or milk**, one spoon at a time.

Tip 8: If you want to use buttercream for piping, **place it in the fridge to cool**, before using.

Recipes: Base Buttercream

American Buttercream

INGREDIENTS:

8 Oz **Butter**, unsalted, softened

2 cups **Sugar**, powdered, sifted

2 tablespoons **Milk**

2 teaspoons **Vanilla**, pure, extract

EQUIPMENT:

Stand or hand mixer fitted with the paddle attachment, Sifter, Food scale or measuring cups set, Cake decorating piping tips and bags (optional).

PREPARATION:

Step 1: Place butter on a kitchen countertop and leave it until it reaches room temperature.

Step 2: In a bowl of stand mixer, fitted with the paddle attachment, beat butter on medium speed, for 2-3 minutes until it becomes soft and light.

Step 3: Gradually add one half of powdered sugar and beat the mixture starting on low speed and continuing on low-medium speed until fully incorporated.

Add vanilla extract. Beat again for 30 seconds.

Slowly add remaining sugar and beat on medium speed until all is fully incorporated and buttercream becomes light and fluffy. Do not overbeat.

Place into the fridge to cool.

Store American Buttercream the refrigerator for up to one week. Beat it with a mixer before using.

Swiss Meringue Buttercream

INGREDIENTS:

12 Oz **Butter**, unsalted, softened

1 cup **Sugar**, powdered, sifted

5 **Egg whites**

1 teaspoon **Vanilla**, pure, extract

¼ teaspoon **Salt**

EQUIPMENT:

Stand or hand mixer fitted with the whisk attachment, Sifter, Heatproof bowl, Food scale or measuring cups set, Cake decorating piping tips and bags (optional).

PREPARATION:

Step 1: Place butter on a kitchen countertop and leave it until it reaches room temperature.

Step 2: Place a heatproof bowl over slowly boiling water bath on low heat. Add egg whites and sugar into the bowl and stir until sugar fully dissolves.

Step 3: Transfer the mixture into a bowl of stand mixer, fitted with the whisk attachment. Beat on medium speed, for 4-5 minutes until meringue becomes thick and glossy.

Step 4: Add softened butter, salt, and vanilla. Beat on medium speed until buttercream becomes silky and smooth.

Place into the fridge to cool.

Store Swiss Meringue Buttercream in the refrigerator for up to one week. Beat it with a mixer before using.

German Buttercream

This buttercream is great as a topping or as a filing. It can be piped to decorate cakes and cupcakes as well.

INGREDIENTS:

8 Oz **Butter**, unsalted, softened

1 cup **Sugar**, cane, granulated

3 **Egg yolks**, large, room temperature

¾ cup **Milk**, whole

1 tablespoon **Cornstarch,** organic (*or **Corn** four*)

1 teaspoon **Vanilla**, pure, extract

¼ teaspoon **Salt**

EQUIPMENT:

Stand or hand mixer fitted with the paddle attachment, Saucepan, Food scale or measuring cups set, Plastic wrap, Cake decorating piping tips and bags (optional).

PREPARATION:

Step 1: Place butter on a kitchen countertop and leave it until it reaches room temperature.

Step 2: In a bowl of stand mixer, fitted with the

paddle attachment, combine half of the granulated sugar, egg yolks, cornstarch, vanilla extract, and salt. Beat it until it becomes a bit foamy. Set it aside.

Step 3: In a saucepan, combine milk and second half of granulated sugar. Heat the mixture over medium-low heat, constantly stirring. Bring it to simmer, and remove from heat.

Step 4: Add half of the hot milk mixture into egg yolk mixture. Beat with a whisk attachment on low speed. Add the remaining hot milk, little by little.

Step 5: Pour this mixture back into the saucepan, over medium-low heat. Stir constantly with a spatula, until the mixture becomes a thick custard. Remove from heat once the mixture starts bubbling.

Step 6: Cover it with plastic wrap and place into the fridge to cool, for approximately two hours.

Step 7: In a bowl of stand mixer, fitted with the paddle attachment, beat butter on medium speed, for 5-7 minutes until it becomes soft and light.

Step 8: Add cooled custard mixture and beat on high speed with a paddle attachment until it becomes creamy and smooth.

Step 9: Add remaining powdered sugar and then

add half of the key lime juice and half of milk and process mixture until smooth.

For the best results, use immediately.

Store German Buttercream in the refrigerator for up to one week. Beat it with a mixer before using.

Vanilla Cream Buttercream

INGREDIENTS:

8 Oz **Butter**, unsalted, softened

4 cups **Sugar**, powdered, sifted

½ cup **Heavy cream**

2 teaspoons **Vanilla**, pure, extract

Pinch of **Salt**

EQUIPMENT:

Stand or hand mixer fitted with the paddle attachment, Sifter, Food scale or measuring cups set, Cake decorating piping tips and bags (optional).

PREPARATION:

Step 1: Place butter on a kitchen countertop and leave it until it reaches room temperature.

Step 2: In a bowl of stand mixer, fitted with the paddle attachment, beat butter on medium speed, for 3-4 minutes until it becomes soft and light.

Step 3: Gradually add one half of powdered sugar and beat starting on low speed and continuing on low-medium speed until fully incorporated.

Add vanilla extract. Beat again for 30 seconds.

Slowly add remaining sugar and beat on medium speed until all is fully incorporated and buttercream becomes light and fluffy. Do not overbeat.

Step 4: Add heavy cream and beat until it reaches desired consistency. Do not overbeat or buttercream will clump.

Place into the fridge to cool.

Store Vanilla Cream Buttercream in the refrigerator for up to one week. Beat it with a mixer before using.

French Buttercream

INGREDIENTS:

16 oz **Butter**, unsalted, softened

8 **Egg yolks**, large, pasteurized

1 cup **Sugar**, cane, granulated

6 tablespoons **Water**

1 teaspoon **Vanilla**, pure, extract

Pinch of **Salt**

EQUIPMENT:

Stand or hand mixer fitted with the paddle attachment, Medium saucepan, Sifter, Food scale or measuring cups set, Cake decorating piping tips and bags (optional).

PREPARATION:

Step 1: Pasteurize egg yolks over the water bath by bringing water to 140°F and simmering for about three minutes. Set aside to cool.

Step 2: Place cooled egg yolks into a bowl of a stand mixer equipped with a whisk attachment. Beat until it becomes thick and foamy.

Step 3: Combine water and sugar in a medium

saucepan. Heat over low-medium heat until sugar dissolves. Once sugar dissolves increase the heat and bring it to boil. Cook the mixture until it reaches 235°F.

Step 4: Start adding hot syrup into the mixing bowl, continuing mixing on low speed. Mix for 5-7 minutes until syrup cools down.

Step 5: Add butter, one tablespoon at a time, into mixing bowl with the cooled mixture. Continue mixing on low speed until butter incorporates and looks creamy.

Add salt and vanilla and mix again for another 1-2 minutes until all is incorporated and becomes smooth and fluffy.

Place in the fridge to cool.

Store French Buttercream in the refrigerator for up to one week. Beat it with a mixer before using.

Italian Meringue Buttercream

This beautiful buttercream can withstand hot temperatures. This buttercream is perfect to stack tiered cakes (such as wedding cakes).

INGREDIENTS:

1 ¼ cups **Sugar**, cane, granulated

2/3 cup **Maple syrup**

2/3 cup **Water**

5 **Egg whites**

1 1/3 cups **Butter,** unsalted, softened

2 2/3 cups **Shortening**, vegetable

2 teaspoons **Vanilla**, pure, extract

EQUIPMENT:

Stand or hand mixer fitted with the paddle attachment, Medium heat-proof bowl, Candy thermometer, Cake decorating piping tips and bags (optional).

PREPARATION:

Step 1: In a heat-proof medium bowl combine sugar, maple syrup, and water. Bring to a boil over medium-high heat. Constantly stir the mixture and heat it to 223°F to 234°F.

The mixture is ready when it forms a soft thread when it is dripped from a spatula. This should take 1 or 2 minutes. Once it is ready, remove it from heat and set aside.

Step 2: Add egg whites into a bowl of stand mixer fitted with the paddle attachment. Beat on low and then on medium speed until it can hold a stiff peak.

Slowly pour sugar syrup mixture in a thin stream, while continuing to whip at a medium speed. Continue mixing for another 10 minutes. Set aside.

Step 3: Add pieces of cold butter one at a time. Continue to beat at medium speed until butter incorporates into the mixture.

Step 4: Add vegetable shortening and continue mixing at a medium speed.

The buttercream will break down and look crumbled. Keep mixing for another 10 minutes until it will become smooth and glossy.

Place into the fridge to cool.

Store Italian Meringue Buttercream in the refrigerator for up to one week. Beat it with a mixer before using.

This recipe contains raw egg. We recommend that pregnant women, young children, the elderly, and the infirm do not consume raw egg.

Buttercream for Flower Piping

INGREDIENTS:

16 Oz **Butter**, unsalted, softened

4 cups **Sugar**, powdered, sifted

¼ cup **Corn flour**, organic *(or Corn starch)*

¼ cup **Cream,** heavy, whipping

2 teaspoons **Vanilla**, pure, extract

1 teaspoon **Salt,** sea

EQUIPMENT:

Stand or hand mixer fitted with the paddle attachment, Sifter, Food scale or measuring cups set, Cake decorating piping tips and bags (optional).

PREPARATION:

Step 1: Place butter and all other ingredients on a kitchen countertop and leave it until it reaches room temperature.

Step 2: In a bowl of stand mixer, fitted with the paddle attachment, beat butter on medium speed, for 2-3 minutes until it becomes soft and light.

Step 3: Add heavy cream, corn flour, and salt. Mix

until all is incorporated to remove any lumps. You may add a bit of powdered sugar to aid the mixing process. Check that all is mixed evenly scraping the bottom of the mixing bowl.

Step 4: Gradually add one-third of powdered sugar and beat starting on low speed and continuing on medium speed until fully incorporated.

Add vanilla extract. Beat again for thirty seconds to one minute.

Slowly add remaining sugar and beat on medium speed until all is fully incorporated and buttercream becomes light and fluffy. Scrape the sides of the bowl and mix again.

Place into the fridge to cool.

Store Buttercream for Flower Piping in the refrigerator for up to one month (or up to 6 months in a freezer). Beat it with a mixer before using.

Notes: if the buttercream is too stiff, add more heavy cream. If it is too liquid, add more powdered sugar. (Both – teaspoon at a time).

Cream Cheese Buttercream

INGREDIENTS:

8 Oz **Butter**, unsalted, softened

8 Oz **Cream cheese,** softened

2 cups **Sugar**, powdered, sifted

1 teaspoon **Vanilla**, pure, extract

EQUIPMENT:

Stand or hand mixer fitted with the paddle attachment, Sifter, Food scale or measuring cups set, Cake decorating piping tips and bags (optional).

PREPARATION:

Step 1: Place butter and cream cheese on a kitchen countertop and leave it until it reaches room temperature.

Step 2: In a bowl of stand mixer, fitted with the paddle attachment, beat cream cheese on medium speed, for 4-5 minutes until it achieved a smooth consistency.

Step 3: Add softened butter, (one quester at a time) and beat on medium speed, for another 5-7 minutes until mixture becomes soft and light.

Step 4: Gradually add one half of powdered sugar and beat starting on low speed and continuing on medium speed until fully incorporated. Add vanilla extract and beat for another 30 seconds to one minute.

Step 5: Add remaining powdered sugar and beat until all is incorporated and buttercream becomes smooth and fluffy.

Place into the fridge to cool.

Store Cream Cheese Buttercream in the refrigerator for up to one week. Beat it with a mixer before using.

Recipes: Fondant & Icing

Rolled Fondant *(Sculpting)*

INGREDIENTS:

8 cups **Sugar**, powdered, sifted

¼ cup **Water**, cold

½ cup **Glucose**, syrup *(from a cake decorating store)*

1 ½ cup **Glycerin** (from a cake decorating store)

1 tablespoon **Gelatin**, unflavored

1 teaspoon **Vanilla**, pure, extract

1 cup **Corn flour**, organic *(to dust your hands and working table)*

EQUIPMENT:

Large mixing bowl, Small saucepan, Measuring cups, Plastic wrap, Rolling pin.

PREPARATION:

Step 1: In a large bowl add sugar, make a well in the center.

Step 2: In a small saucepan add cold water and gelatin. Set aside for five minutes.

Transfer the mixture into the oven and heat it until the gelatin dissolves. Do not boil. Set aside, add glycerin, vanilla extract, and glucose syrup. Mix well.

Step 3: Pour the mixture into the sugar well. Start folding sugar into the mixture and mix it until all is well incorporated.

Knead the icing with your hands until it becomes stiff. If the mixture is too runny add more powdered sugar.

Step 4: Roll the icing into a ball, cover with a plastic wrap, and place into an airtight container. Place on a countertop and set aside for about seven to eight hours.

After 7-8 hours rolled fondant is ready to use. Roll fondant with a rolling pin into a thin layer to cover your cake.

Do not refrigerate. Rolled Fondant will keep fresh for two days at a room temperature.

Rolled Fondant *(Gum Paste)*

INGREDIENTS:

8 cups **Sugar**, powdered, sifted

½ cup **Egg whites,** pasteurized

3 tablespoons **Tylose**, powder *(from a specialty cake decorating store)*

2 tablespoons **Vegetable shortening**

1 teaspoon **Vanilla**, pure, extract

1 cup **Corn flour**, organic *(to dust your hands and working table)*

EQUIPMENT:

Small saucepan, Small mixing bowl, Measuring cups, Stand mixer.

PREPARATION:

Step 1: Pasteurize egg whites by placing them in a water bath and heating water to 138°F, then simmering for four minutes.

Step 2: In a bowl of a stand mixer add egg whites and beat them with a paddle attachment for about 8 to 10 minutes.

Step 3: Add powdered sugar, little by little mixing on a low speed. Once all powdered sugar is incorporated, turn up the mixer speed and beat for several minutes until mixture forms soft peaks.

The mixture should be thick and glossy like a meringue. Mix eggs and sugar enough to form a think mixture or your fondant will be too liquid.

Step 4: Add tylose and mix on a low speed to incorporate. Turn mixer up and blend until the mixture thickens.

Store Gum Paste in a zip-lock bag, without any access air, in an airtight container. Do not refrigerate.

Poured Fondant

INGREDIENTS:

8 cups **Sugar**, powdered, sifted

¼ cup **Water**, cold

¼ cup **Glucose**, syrup *(from a cake decorating store)*

1 teaspoon **Vanilla**, pure, extract

EQUIPMENT:

Large mixing bowl, Small saucepan, Measuring cups, Plastic wrap, Rolling pin.

PREPARATION:

Step 1: Sift in powdered sugar, add water and glucose syrup into a large saucepan.

Place on stove on low heat and warm the mixture up to 90°F. Set aside and add vanilla extract.

Make sure the mixture is liquid enough to pour over the cake and thick another to coat the cake.

Store in in the fridge in an airtight container. Reheat to 100°F before using.

Marzipan Icing

Marzipan Icing is great for Christmas cakes and candies.

INGREDIENTS:

12 Oz **Almonds**, blanched, finely ground

2 cups **Sugar**, powdered, sifted

2 **Egg whites,** pasteurized

1 teaspoon **Almond**, pure, extract

¼ teaspoon **Salt**

EQUIPMENT:

Stand or hand mixer fitted with the paddle attachment, Plastic wrap, Cake decorating piping tips and bags (optional).

PREPARATION:

Step 1: In a bowl of stand mixer, fitted with the paddle attachment, combine, powdered sugar and egg whites. Beat on medium speed until mixture becomes smooth and foamy.

Step 2: Add finely ground almonds, salt and almond extract and beat on medium speed until perfectly blended.

Cover with plastic wrap and leave in a fridge for 24 hours to harden.

Place into the fridge to cool.

Store Marzipan Icing in the refrigerator for up to one week.

This recipe contains raw egg. We recommend that pregnant women, young children, the elderly, and the infirm do not consume raw egg.

Tip: You can pasteurize eggs by heating an egg to 138°F and then cooling.

Royal Icing

INGREDIENTS:

2 **Egg whites**, pasteurized

4 cups **Sugar**, powdered

1 tablespoon **Lemon juice**

EQUIPMENT:

Stand or hand mixer fitted with the paddle attachment, Food scale or measuring cups set, Cake decorating piping tips and bags (optional).

PREPARATION:

Step 1: In a bowl of stand mixer, fitted with the paddle attachment, combine egg whites and lemon juice. Add two tablespoons of powdered sugar. Mix on low speed, then on medium speed.

Step 2: Little by little, keep adding powdered sugar. Keep beating until mixture starts looking like heavy whipped cream and when it "freezes" when you pull up the mixer's paddle attachment.
Place into the fridge to cool.

Store Royal Icing in the refrigerator for up to one week, covered in a plastic wrap. Beat it with a mixer before using.

Chocolate Ganache

INGREDIENTS:

8 Oz **Chocolate,** dark, bakers

8 Oz **Cream,** heavy

1 teaspoon **Vanilla**, pure, extract

EQUIPMENT:

Medium size saucepan, Medium bowl, Food scale or measuring cups set, Whisk, Cake decorating piping tips and bags (optional).

PREPARATION:

Step 1: In a saucepan, over low heat, bring heavy cream to simmer.

Remove from heat.

Step 2: Break the dark chocolate into pieces and place them into a medium mixing bowl. Pour hot heavy cream over the chocolate and whisk it until smooth.

Place into the fridge to cool.

At first, the mixture may be too liquid. Ganache will firm up when it sets.

Depending on your goal, you can use this chocolate ganache to drizzle over your cakes or cupcakes while it is still very liquid, or wait until it sets a bit and cover an entire cake or cupcakes. You can also use it as filling for chocolate candies.

Store Chocolate Ganache in the refrigerator for up to one week. Beat it with a mixer before using.

Quick and Simple Buttercream

This is a great "base" buttercream.

INGREDIENTS:

4 Oz **Butter**, unsalted, softened

2 cups **Sugar**, cane, powdered

2 tablespoons Milk, whole

1 teaspoon **Vanilla**, pure, extract

1 teaspoon **Almond**, pure, extract

EQUIPMENT:

Stand or hand mixer fitted with the paddle attachment, Cake decorating piping tips and bags (optional).

PREPARATION:

Step 1: Place butter on a kitchen countertop and leave it until it reaches room temperature.

Step 2: In a bowl of stand mixer, fitted with the paddle attachment, add butter and beat it at medium speed until it becomes smooth and fluffy.

Step 3: Gradually add powdered sugar and beat until it is fully incorporated. Add vanilla extract and beat for another 30 seconds.

Step 4: Add milk and beat for another 45 seconds. Do not overbeat.

Place into the fridge to cool.

Store Quick and Simple Buttercream in the refrigerator for up to one week. Beat it with a mixer before using.

Recipes: Flavoured Buttercream

German Chocolate Buttercream

Amazing buttercream for German Chocolate Cake.

INGREDIENTS:

8 Oz **Butter**, softened

3 **Egg yolks**

1 1/3 cups **Coconut**, shredded, unsweetened

1 cup **Sugar**, brown

1 cup **Milk**, evaporated

1 cup **Pecans**, roasted, chopped

1 teaspoon **Vanilla**, pure, extract

EQUIPMENT:

Stand or hand mixer fitted with the paddle attachment, Large saucepan, Cake decorating piping tips and bags (optional).

PREPARATION:

Step 1: Place butter on a kitchen countertop and leave it until it reaches room temperature.

Step 2: In a large saucepan combine evaporated

milk, brown sugar, egg yolks, butter, and vanilla. Cook over low heat, constantly stirring until mixture is thick.

Remove from heat and stir in pecans and coconut. Set aside and let it cool to room temperature.

Step 3: In a bowl of stand mixer, fitted with the paddle attachment, add softened butter and beat it at medium speed until it becomes smooth.

Step 4: Little by little, add cooled mixture and beat it on low to medium speed until all is incorporated and becomes smooth and fluffy.

Place into the fridge to cool.

Store German Chocolate Buttercream in the refrigerator for up to one week. Beat it with a mixer before using.

Almond Buttercream

This buttercream is perfect for cookies and cupcakes.

INGREDIENTS:

4 cups **Sugar**, powdered

1 cup **Butter**, unsalted, softened

1 cup **Shortening**, vegetable

4 1/2 tablespoons **Milk**

1 1/2 teaspoons **Almond**, extract

EQUIPMENT:

Stand or hand mixer fitted with the paddle attachment, Cake decorating piping tips and bags (optional).

PREPARATION:

Step 1: Place butter on a kitchen countertop and leave it until it reaches room temperature.

Step 2: In a bowl of stand mixer, fitted with the paddle attachment, combine softened butter and shortening, and beat it at medium speed for 3-4 minutes.

Add almond extract and beat for another 45

seconds.

Step 3: Add powdered sugar, one cup at a time. In between, add in milk, one tablespoon at a time. Mix for 30 seconds to 45 seconds until buttercream becomes creamy and smooth.

Place into the fridge to cool.

Store Almond Buttercream in the refrigerator for up to one week. Beat it with a mixer before using.

Banana Buttercream

This buttercream is light and fluffy. It is great for chocolate cakes and cupcakes.

INGREDIENTS:

8 Oz **Whipped topping**, frozen, thawed

3.5 Oz **Banana pudding**, instant, mix

1 **Banana**, very ripe, mashed

1 cup **Milk**

2 tablespoons **Rum**

EQUIPMENT:

Stand or hand mixer fitted with the paddle attachment, Cake decorating piping tips and bags (optional).

PREPARATION:

Step 1: In a bowl of stand mixer, fitted with the paddle attachment, combine banana pudding, mashed banana, milk, and rum.

Beat on a low to medium speed until mixture becomes very thick.

Step 2: Gently beat in thawed whipped topping. Continue to beat until it becomes smooth.

Place into the fridge to cool.

Store Banana Buttercream in the refrigerator for up to one week. Beat it with a mixer before using.

Paradise Island Buttercream

Perfect buttercream for cakes with condensed milk or chocolate cakes.

INGREDIENTS:

2 cups **Sugar**, powdered

2 cups **Butter**, unsalted, softened

1 cup **Condensed milk**, sweetened

EQUIPMENT:

Stand or hand mixer fitted with the paddle attachment, Cake decorating piping tips and bags (optional).

PREPARATION:

Step 1: Place butter on a kitchen countertop and leave it until it reaches room temperature.

Step 2: In a bowl of stand mixer, fitted with the paddle attachment, beat softened butter at medium speed, until it becomes smooth and fluffy.

Step 3: Gradually beat in powdered sugar until it becomes fully incorporated.

Step 4: Add condensed milk, continue beating until smooth.

Place into the fridge to cool.

Store Paradise Island Buttercream in the refrigerator for up to one week. Beat it with a mixer before using.

Caramel Dreams Buttercream

This caramel buttercream is wonderful for chocolate cakes.

INGREDIENTS:

1 cup **Sugar**, brown

1/3 cup **Milk**

2 tablespoons **Butter**, unsalted, softened

1 tablespoon **Cream**, heavy

1 teaspoon **Vanilla**, pure, extract

1/8 teaspoon **Salt**

EQUIPMENT:

Stand or hand mixer fitted with the paddle attachment, Large saucepan, Cake decorating piping tips and bags (optional).

PREPARATION:

Step 1: In a large saucepan, combine brown sugar, salt, butter, and milk. Cook over medium heat, stirring until the mixture comes to a boil and sugar dissolves.

Cool to lukewarm (110°F).

Step 2: Transfer the mixture into a bowl of stand mixer and beat until it begins to thicken.

Add vanilla and heavy cream and beat for another 30-45 seconds until frosting becomes smooth.

Place into the fridge to cool.

Store Caramel Dreams Buttercream in the refrigerator for up to one week. Beat it with a mixer before using.

Go Nuts Cream Cheese Buttercream

Great buttercream for chocolate cakes.

INGREDIENTS:

8 Oz **Cream cheese**, softened

4 Oz **Butter**, unsalted, softened

4 cups **Sugar**, powdered

1 cup **Pecans**, chopped

EQUIPMENT:

Stand or hand mixer fitted with the paddle attachment, Cake decorating piping tips and bags (optional).

PREPARATION:

Step 1: Place butter and cream cheese on a kitchen countertop and leave it until it reaches room temperature.

Step 2: In a bowl of stand mixer, fitted with the paddle attachment, beat cream cheese on medium speed, for 3-4 minutes until it becomes soft and fluffy.

Step 3: Little by little add softened butter and beat on medium speed until all is incorporated and fluffy.

Step 4: Add powdered sugar and vanilla. Beat until creamy and add chopped nuts. Mix for another 45 seconds.

Place into the fridge to cool.

Store Go Nuts Cream Cheese Buttercream in the refrigerator for up to one week. Beat it with a mixer before using.

Hazelnut Buttercream

This frosting is wonderful for chocolate cakes.

INGREDIENTS:

8 Oz **Cream cheese**, softened

4 Oz cup **Butter**, unsalted, softened

1 cup **Chocolate-hazelnut**, spread

1 tablespoon **Milk**

EQUIPMENT:

Stand or hand mixer fitted with the paddle attachment, Cake decorating piping tips and bags (optional).

PREPARATION:

Step 1: Place butter and cream cheese on a kitchen countertop and leave it until it reaches room temperature.

Step 2: In a bowl of stand mixer, fitted with the paddle attachment, beat cream cheese on medium speed, for 4-5 minutes until it becomes soft and fluffy.

Step 3: Little by little add softened butter and beat on medium speed until all is incorporated and fluffy.

Step 4: Add hazelnut spread and milk and continue beating until smooth and fluffy.

Place into the fridge to cool.

Store Hazelnut Buttercream in the refrigerator for up to one week. Beat it with a mixer before using.

Cream Cheese Dream Buttercream

Great buttercream for pumpkin bread, carrot cake and chocolate cake.

INGREDIENTS:

16 Oz **Cream cheese**, softened

4 Oz **Butter**, unsalted, softened

4 cups **Sugar**, cane, powdered

1 teaspoon **Vanilla**, pure, extract

EQUIPMENT:

Stand or hand mixer fitted with the paddle attachment, Cake decorating piping tips and bags (optional).

PREPARATION:

Step 1: Place butter and cream cheese on a kitchen countertop and leave it until it reaches room temperature.

Step 2: In a bowl of stand mixer, fitted with the paddle attachment, add cream cheese and beat it at medium speed until it becomes smooth.

Little by little, add softened butter and continue mixing until it becomes smooth and fluffy.

Step 3: Add vanilla extract, gradually add powdered sugar. Beat on medium speed until buttercream becomes light and fluffy.

Place into the fridge to cool.

Store Cream Cheese Dream Buttercream in the refrigerator for up to one week. Beat it with a mixer before using.

Lemon Cream Cheese Buttercream

This Lemon Cream Cheese Buttercream is perfect for lemon drops.

INGREDIENTS:

4 Oz **Cream cheese**, softened

4 Oz **Butter**, unsalted, softened

2 ¼ cups **Sugar**, cane, powdered *and*

1 cup **Sugar**, cane, powdered

2 tablespoons **Lemon juice**

EQUIPMENT:

Stand or hand mixer fitted with the paddle attachment, Medium mixing bowl, Cake decorating piping tips and bags (optional).

PREPARATION:

Step 1: Place butter and cream cheese on a kitchen countertop and leave it until it reaches room temperature.

Step 2: In a bowl of stand mixer, fitted with the paddle attachment, add cream cheese and beat it at medium speed until it becomes smooth.

Little by little, add softened butter and continue mixing until it becomes smooth and fluffy.

Step 3: Add one cup of powdered sugar and lemon juice and beat for 30 seconds.

Step 4: Little by little, add the remaining 2 ¼ cups of powdered sugar. Beat until buttercream becomes creamy and light.

Place into the fridge to cool.

Store Lemon Cream Buttercream in the refrigerator for up to one week. Beat it with a mixer before using.

Chocolate Marshmallow Fondant

Very good chocolate fondant to cover chocolate cakes.

INGREDIENTS:

16 Oz **Marshmallow**s, miniature

4 cups **Sugar**, powdered

1/2 cup **Chocolate chips**, dark, bakers

2 tablespoons **Maple syrup**

1 teaspoon **Coffee**, extract

EQUIPMENT:

Two small heat proof bowls, Plastic wrap.

PREPARATION:

Step 1: In a small bowl, melt marshmallows on a water bath, constantly stirring. Add maple syrup and coffee-flavored extract.

Step 2: In a small bowl, melt chocolate chips over a water bath, constantly stirring.

Step 3. Fold chocolate mixture into the marshmallow mixture.

Step 4: Add powdered sugar, one cup at a time,

into the chocolate-marshmallow mixture, until a thick, stringy dough forms.

Step 5: Add some powdered sugar on a flat working surface, turn dough out and knead until smooth and no longer sticky.

Step 6: Wrap tightly in plastic wrap. Let fondant rest at room temperature, from eight hours to overnight.

Store Chocolate Marshmallow Fondant in the refrigerator for up to one week.

Snow White Buttercream

This simple buttercream is good for any kind of cupcakes or cakes.

INGREDIENTS:

1 cup **Sugar**, cane, powdered

1/2 cup **Butter**, unsalted, softened

1/2 cup **Shortening**, vegetable

1/4 cup **Flour**, all-purpose

1 cup **Milk**

1 teaspoon **Vanilla**, pure, extract

EQUIPMENT:

Stand or hand mixer fitted with the paddle attachment, Small saucepan, Cake decorating piping tips and bags (optional).

PREPARATION:

Step 1: In a small saucepan, combine milk and flour. Cook over medium-high heat until mixture is boiling. Remove from heat and set aside to cool.

Step 2: In a bowl of stand mixer, fitted with the paddle attachment, beat softened butter on medium speed, for 3-4 minutes until it becomes soft and fluffy. Slowly add powdered sugar and beat on slow speed first until all is fully incorporated.

Step 3: Add vegetable shortening and vanilla. Beat on medium speed for a minute.

Step 4: Transfer cooled mixture into the bowl with buttercream and beat on medium speed until all is fully incorporated.

Place into the fridge to cool.

Store Snow White Buttercream in the refrigerator for up to one week. Beat it with a mixer before using.

Christmas Eggnog Buttercream

This is a great buttercream to decorate holiday cakes and cupcakes.

INGREDIENTS:

4 cups **Sugar**, powdered

4 Oz **Butter**, unsalted, softened

6 tablespoons **Eggnog**

1 teaspoon **Vanilla**, pure, extract

EQUIPMENT:

Stand or hand mixer fitted with the paddle attachment, Cake decorating piping tips and bags (optional).

PREPARATION:

Step 1: Place butter and on a kitchen countertop and leave it until it reaches room temperature.

Step 2: In a bowl of stand mixer, fitted with the paddle attachment, beat butter on medium speed, for 3-4 minutes until it becomes soft and light.

Step 3: Add eggnog and vanilla extract. Beat on medium speed until all is well combined.

Step 4: Slowly add powdered sugar. Keep beating

until the mixture becomes soft and fluffy.

Place into the fridge to cool.

Store Christmas Eggnog Buttercream in the refrigerator for up to one week. Beat it with a mixer before using.

Raspberry Buttercream

Perfect buttercream for any cake that calls for a fruity flavor.

INGREDIENTS:

FOR THE BUTTERCREAM:

2 cups **Sugar**, powdered

1 cup **Butter**, unsalted, softened

1 teaspoon **Vanilla**, pure, extract

For the Raspberry Puree:

1 cup **Raspberries**, fresh or frozen, thawed

2 tablespoons **Cream,** heavy, whipping

EQUIPMENT:

Stand or hand mixer fitted with the paddle attachment, Cake decorating piping tips and bags (optional).

PREPARATION:

MAKE THE PUREE:

Step 1: In a blender, puree raspberries and heavy cream until smooth.

Transfer into a small saucepan, add two tablespoons of powdered sugar and reduce the liquid by simmering over low heat. Set aside to cool.

MAKE THE BUTTERCREAM:

Step 1: Place butter and on a kitchen countertop and leave it until it reaches room temperature.

Step 2: In a bowl of stand mixer, fitted with the paddle attachment, beat butter on medium speed, for 3-4 minutes until it becomes soft and light.

Step 3: Gradually add powdered sugar and beat until fully incorporated. Add vanilla extract and beat again for 30 seconds.

Step 4: Add raspberries puree and beat for another 45 seconds. Do not overbeat.

Place into the fridge to cool.

Store Raspberry Buttercream in the refrigerator for up to one week. Beat it with a mixer before using.

Black Volcano Buttercream

Great buttercream icing for chocolate or caramel cakes.

INGREDIENTS:

12 Oz **Condensed milk**, sweetened

8 Oz **Butter**, unsalted, softened

2 cups **Sugar**, powdered

1/2 cup **Cocoa powder**, Dutch, unsweetened

1 teaspoon **Vanilla**, pure, extract

EQUIPMENT:

Stand or hand mixer fitted with the paddle attachment, Cake decorating piping tips and bags (optional).

PREPARATION:

Step 1: Place butter and on a kitchen countertop and leave it until it reaches room temperature.

Step 2: In a bowl of stand mixer, fitted with the paddle attachment, beat butter on medium speed, for 3-4 minutes until it becomes soft and light.

Step 3: Gradually add powdered sugar and beat until fully incorporated. Add vanilla extract and beat again for 30 seconds.

Step 4: Add condensed milk and cocoa powder and beat until smooth. Do not overbeat.

Place into the fridge to cool.

Store Black Volcano Buttercream in the refrigerator for up to one week. Beat it with a mixer before using.

Morning Joy Coffee Buttercream

This coffee buttercream is wonderful for coffee lovers. Works great with chocolate and caramel cakes.

INGREDIENTS:

4 Oz **Butter**, unsalted, softened

2 cups **Sugar**, powdered

1 tablespoon **Cocoa powder**, unsweetened

1 tablespoon **Coffee**, strong brewed

EQUIPMENT:

Stand or hand mixer fitted with the paddle attachment, Small mixing bowl, Cake decorating piping tips and bags (optional).

PREPARATION:

Step 1: In a small bowl, stir together powdered sugar and cocoa powder. Set aside.

Step 2: In a bowl of stand mixer fitted with the paddle attachment add butter and beat it at a medium speed until creamy.

Gradually add sugar and cocoa powder mixture, and beat until smooth at medium speed for 30-45 seconds.

Step 3: Stir in the coffee, and beat until smooth for another 30 seconds.

Place into the fridge to cool.

Store Morning Joy Coffee Buttercream in the refrigerator for up to one week. Beat it with a mixer before using.

Amaretto-Maple Cream Cheese Buttercream

Good buttercream for many kinds of cakes, including, chocolate cakes.

INGREDIENTS:

8 Oz cream cheese, softened

4 Oz **Butter**, unsalted, softened

2 ½ cups Sugar, powdered

1/4 cup **Amaretto liqueur**

1 tablespoon **Maple syrup**, pure

1/2 teaspoon **Vanilla**, pure, extract

EQUIPMENT:

Stand or hand mixer fitted with the paddle attachment, Cake decorating piping tips and bags (optional).

PREPARATION:

Step 1: Place butter and cream cheese on a kitchen countertop and leave it until it reaches room temperature.

Step 2: In a bowl of stand mixer, fitted with the paddle attachment, beat cream cheese on medium speed, for 5-7 minutes until it becomes soft and fluffy.

Step 3: Little by little add softened butter and beat on medium speed until all is incorporated and fluffy.

Step 4: Add powdered sugar, amaretto liqueur, maple syrup, and vanilla extract. Beat until smooth and fluffy.

Place into the fridge to cool.

Store Amaretto Maple-Cream Cheese Buttercream in the refrigerator for up to one week. Beat it with a mixer before using.

Avocado Buttercream

This is a lighter version of buttercream. Great for carrot cupcakes.

INGREDIENTS:

2 cups **Sugar**, powdered

8 Oz **Avocado**, meat of *(approx. 2 avocados)*

2 teaspoons **Lemon juice**, freshly squeezed

1/2 teaspoon **Lemon**, extract

EQUIPMENT:

Stand or hand mixer fitted with the paddle attachment, Cake decorating piping tips and bags (optional).

PREPARATION:

Step 1: Peel and pit the avocados. Place avocado meat into a bowl of stand mixer, add lemon juice and beat for 2 to 3 minutes until it lightens in color.

Step 2: Add powdered sugar, little at a time, and beat until smooth. Add the lemon extract and beat for another 30 seconds to combine.

Place into the fridge to cool.

Store Avocado Buttercream in the refrigerator for up to

one week. Beat it with a mixer before using.

Champagne Buttercream

Surprise your guests with champagne buttercream decorated cakes or cupcakes.

INGREDIENTS:

8 Oz **butter**, unsalted, softened

3 cups **Sugar**, powdered

4 tablespoons **Champagne**

EQUIPMENT:

Stand or hand mixer fitted with the paddle attachment, Cake decorating piping tips and bags (optional).

PREPARATION:

Step 1: Place butter on a kitchen countertop and leave it until it reaches room temperature.

Step 2: In a bowl of stand mixer, fitted with the paddle attachment, beat butter on medium speed, for 5-7 minutes until it becomes soft and light.

Step 3: Gradually add powdered sugar and beat until fully incorporated. Add vanilla extract and beat again for 30 seconds.

Step 4: Add Champagne and mix until it is evenly

incorporated and frosting is smooth and creamy.

Place into the fridge to cool.

Store Champagne Buttercream in the refrigerator for up to one week. Beat it with a mixer before using.

White Chocolate Buttercream

INGREDIENTS:

8 Oz **Butter**, unsalted, softened

8 Oz **Chocolate**, white, bakers

1 teaspoon **Vanilla**, pure, extract

EQUIPMENT:

Stand or hand mixer fitted with the paddle attachment, Food scale or measuring cups set, Medium saucepan, Cake decorating piping tips and bags (optional).

PREPARATION:

Step 1: Combine butter and white chocolate in a medium saucepan. Place it over low heat constantly stirring the mixture. When butter and chocolate are fully melted remove saucepan from heat.

Step 2: Set aside the mixture in room temperature for 20-30 minutes. When the mixture cools off to room temperature, place saucepan into the fridge and refrigerate for about three hours.

Step 3: After three hours, remove frosting from the fridge and let it sit at room temperature for 30 to 45 minutes.

Step 4: Transfer the buttercream into a bowl of stand mixer, fitted with the paddle attachment. Add vanilla extract. Beat the mixture on medium speed, for 5-7 minutes until it becomes soft and light.

Place into the fridge to cool.

Store White Chocolate Buttercream in the refrigerator for up to one week. Beat it with a mixer before using.

Strawberry Cream Cheese Frosting

Good buttercream for many kinds of cakes, including, chocolate or white cakes.

INGREDIENTS:

4 Oz **Cream cheese**, softened

4 Oz **Butter**, unsalted, softened

1 1/4 cups **Sugar**, powdered

1/2 cup **Cream**, heavy whipping

1/4 cup **Strawberry**, puree

1/2 teaspoon **Vanilla**, pure extract

EQUIPMENT:

Stand or hand mixer fitted with the paddle attachment, Cake decorating piping tips and bags (optional).

PREPARATION:

Step 1: Place butter and cream cheese on a kitchen countertop and leave it until it reaches room temperature.

Step 2: Chill a large glass or metal bowl and the beaters for 30 minutes.

Step 3: In a large chilled bowl of a stand mixer, beat heavy whipping cream on medium speed, for 5-6 minutes, until stiff peaks start to form.

Step 4: In a separate bowl, beat cream cheese, for 1-2 minutes, until creamy.

Step 5: Add softened butter and continue beating on medium speed, for 3-4 minutes, until it becomes well blended and smooth.

Step 6: Add strawberry puree and vanilla extract. Beat for another 2-3 minutes. Add powdered sugar and beat for 4-5 minutes until it is soft and fluffy.

Step 7: Fold in the whipped cream into the cream cheese mixture until whipped cream is evenly incorporated.

Place into the fridge to cool.

Store Strawberry Cream Cheese Frosting in the refrigerator for up to 1 week. Beat it with a mixer before using.

Dark Chocolate Buttercream

INGREDIENTS:

8 Oz **Butter,** unsalted, softened

8 Oz **Chocolate,** dark, bakers

1 teaspoon **Vanilla,** pure, extract

EQUIPMENT:

Stand or hand mixer fitted with the paddle attachment, Food scale or measuring cups set, Medium saucepan, Cake decorating piping tips and bags (optional).

PREPARATION:

Step 1: Combine butter and dark chocolate in a medium saucepan. Place it over low heat constantly stirring the mixture. When butter and chocolate are fully melted remove saucepan from the heat.

Step 2: Set aside for 20-30 minutes in room temperature. When the mixture cools off, place saucepan into the fridge and refrigerate for about three hours.

Step 3: After three hours, remove frosting from the fridge and let it sit at room temperature for 30 to 45 minutes.

Step 4: Transfer into a bowl of stand mixer, fitted with the paddle attachment. Add vanilla extract. Beat the chocolate mixture on medium speed, for 5-7 minutes until it becomes soft and light.

Place into the fridge to cool.

Store Dark Chocolate Buttercream in the refrigerator for up to one week. Beat it with a mixer before using.

White Chocolate Glaze

INGREDIENTS:

6 Oz **Chocolate**, white, bakers

¼ cup **Heavy**, cream

1 teaspoon **Vanilla**, pure, extract

EQUIPMENT:

Hand whisk, Food scale or measuring cups set, Medium heatproof bowl, Medium saucepan, Cake decorating piping tips and bags (optional).

PREPARATION:

Step 1: Place finely chopped white chocolate into a small heatproof bowl. Set over a warm water bath on low heat. Stir until chocolate melts.

Remove from the heat and stir until smooth.

Step 2: In a small saucepan, heat heavy cream over low heat, constantly stirring until it starts simmering.

Remove from heat. Add 2/3 of hot heavy cream into the bowl with melted white chocolate.

Gently mix it to incorporate gradually adding

remaining heavy cream.

Step 3: Beat with a whisk until smooth.

Place into the fridge to cool.

Store in the refrigerator for up to 1 week. Beat it with a mixer before using.

Vanilla Buttercream

INGREDIENTS:

8 Oz **Butter**, unsalted, softened

1 cup **Sugar**, powdered, sifter

2 tablespoons **Milk,** whole

2 teaspoons **Vanilla**, pure, extract

1 **Vanilla Bean**, pod, seeds

¼ teaspoon **Salt**

EQUIPMENT:

Stand or hand mixer fitted with the paddle attachment, Sifter, Food scale or measuring cups set, Cake decorating piping tips and bags (optional).

PREPARATION:

Step 1: Place butter on a kitchen countertop and leave it until it reaches room temperature.

Step 2: In a bowl of stand mixer, fitted with the paddle attachment, beat butter on medium speed, for 3-4 minutes until it becomes soft and light.

Step 3: Gradually add one half of powdered sugar and beat starting on low speed and continuing on medium speed until fully incorporated.

Add vanilla extract, vanilla bean seeds, and salt. Beat again for 30 seconds.

Step 4: Slowly add remaining sugar and beat on medium speed until all is fully incorporated and buttercream becomes light and fluffy.

Place into the fridge to cool.

Store Vanilla Buttercream in the refrigerator for up to one week. Beat it with a mixer before using.

Amaretto Buttercream

INGREDIENTS:

8 Oz **Butter**, unsalted, softened

2 cups **Sugar**, powdered, sifted

2 tablespoons **Cream,** heavy

3 tablespoons **Amaretto,** liquor

EQUIPMENT:

Stand or hand mixer fitted with the paddle attachment, Sifter, Food scale or measuring cups set, Cake decorating piping tips and bags (optional).

PREPARATION:

Step 1: Place butter on a kitchen countertop and leave it until it reaches room temperature.

Step 2: In a bowl of stand mixer, fitted with the paddle attachment, beat butter on medium speed, for 3-4 minutes until it becomes soft and light.

Step 3: Gradually add one half of powdered sugar and beat starting on low speed and continuing on medium speed until fully incorporated. Add Amaretto liquor and beat for another 30 seconds.

Step 4: Add remaining powdered sugar and beat until all is incorporated and buttercream becomes smooth and fluffy.

Place into the fridge to cool.

Store Amaretto Buttercream in the refrigerator for up to one week. Beat it with a mixer before using.

Marshmallow Fluff Buttercream

INGREDIENTS:

8 Oz **Butter**, unsalted, softened

2 cups **Sugar**, powdered, sifted

1 cup **Marshmallow,** fluff

1 teaspoon **Vanilla**, pure, extract

¼ teaspoon **Salt**

EQUIPMENT:

Stand or hand mixer fitted with the paddle attachment, Sifter, Food scale or measuring cups set, Cake decorating piping tips and bags (optional).

PREPARATION:

Step 1: Place butter and on a kitchen countertop and leave it until it reaches room temperature.

Step 2: In a bowl of stand mixer, fitted with the paddle attachment, beat butter on medium speed, for 4-5 minutes until it becomes light and smooth.

Step 3: Gradually add 1/4 of powdered sugar and beat it starting on low speed and continuing on medium speed until fully incorporated. Add marshmallow fluff and beat the mixture for another 5 minutes.

Add vanilla extract and salt. Beat for another 1-2 minutes.

Step 4: Add remaining powdered sugar and beat for 3-4 minutes until all is incorporated and buttercream becomes smooth and fluffy.

Place into the fridge to cool.

Store Marshmallow Fluff Buttercream in the refrigerator for up to one week. Beat it with a mixer before using.

Silver Mountain Buttercream

This is a very good frosting for any kind of cakes.

INGREDIENTS:

3 cups **Sugar**, powdered

3 **Egg whites,** pasteurized

1 cup **Water**

1/4 teaspoon **Cream of tartar**

1 teaspoon **Vanilla**, pure, extract

EQUIPMENT:

Stand or hand mixer fitted with the paddle attachment, Large saucepan, Candy thermometer, Cake decorating piping tips and bags (optional).

PREPARATION:

Step 1: In a large saucepan, combine sugar, water, and cream of tartar. Cook until 238°F (measure with a candy thermometer) or until syrup spins a long thread when dripped from a spatula.

Set aside to cool slightly.

Step 2: In a bowl of stand mixer, fitted with the paddle attachment, beat egg whites until stiff.

Step 3: Pour a slow stream of syrup into egg whites, beating constantly, until frosting stands in peaks.

Add in vanilla extract and beat for another 30 seconds.

Place into the fridge to cool.

Store Silver Mountain Buttercream in the refrigerator for up to one week. Beat it with a mixer before using.

This recipe contains raw egg. We recommend that pregnant women, young children, the elderly, and the infirm do not consume raw egg.

Tip: If a recipe uses raw eggs, you can pasteurize eggs by heating an egg to 138°F and then cooling.

Peanut Butter Buttercream

INGREDIENTS:

8 Oz **Peanut butter**, unsalted, softened

6 Oz **Butter**, unsalted, softened

2 cups **Sugar**, powdered, sifted

1 teaspoon **Vanilla**, pure, extract

EQUIPMENT:

Stand or hand mixer fitted with the paddle attachment, Sifter, Food scale or measuring cups set, Cake decorating piping tips and bags (optional).

PREPARATION:

Step 1: Place butter and peanut butter on a kitchen countertop and leave it until it reaches room temperature.

Step 2: In a bowl of stand mixer, fitted with the paddle attachment, beat butter on medium speed, for 3-4 minutes until it becomes light and smooth.

Step 3: Add peanut butter (one quarter at a time) and beat on medium speed until it is fully incorporated.

Step 4: Gradually add one half of powdered sugar and beat starting on low speed and continuing on medium speed until all is fully incorporated.

Add vanilla extract and beat for another 30 seconds.

Step 5: Add remaining powdered sugar and beat until all is incorporated and buttercream becomes smooth and fluffy. Do not overbeat.

Place into the fridge to cool.

Store Peanut Butter Buttercream in the refrigerator for up to one week. Beat it with a mixer before using.

Caramel Buttercream

INGREDIENTS:

4 Oz **Butter**, unsalted, softened

1 ½ cups **Sugar**, powdered, sifted

1 cup **Sugar**, brown

¼ cup **Cream**, heavy

1 teaspoon **Vanilla**, pure, extract

¼ teaspoon **Salt**

EQUIPMENT:

Stand or hand mixer fitted with the paddle attachment, Medium size saucepan, Sifter, Food scale or measuring cups set, Cake decorating piping tips and bags (optional).

PREPARATION:

Step 1: Melt butter in a saucepan over low heat. Add brown sugar and heavy cream. Cook the mixture, stirring, until the mixture starts bubbling and smells like caramel.

Remove from heat. Add vanilla extract and salt. Let it cool for a few minutes.

Step 2: Transfer caramel into a bowl of stand mixer. Add 1/4 of powdered sugar. Beat the mixture on low speed until all is fully incorporated, then increase speed to medium.

Add vanilla extract and salt. Beat for another 1-2 minutes.

Step 3: Little by little, keep adding the rest of powdered sugar and beat until all is incorporated and the mixture is smooth and light.

Place into the fridge to cool.

Store Caramel Buttercream in the refrigerator for up to one week. Beat it with a mixer before using.

Blueberry Buttercream

INGREDIENTS:

FOR THE BUTTERCREAM:

8 Oz **Butter**, unsalted, softened

2 cups **Sugar**, powdered, sifted

1 teaspoon **Vanilla**, pure, extract

FOR THE BLUEBERRIES PUREE:

1 cup **Blueberries**, frozen, thawed

2 tablespoons **Milk,** whole

EQUIPMENT:

Stand or hand mixer fitted with a paddle attachment, Blender or food processor, Small saucepan, Food scale or measuring cups set, Sifter, Cake decorating piping tips and bags (optional).

PREPARATION:

MAKE THE PUREE:

Step 1: In a blender, puree blueberries and heavy cream until smooth.

Transfer into a small saucepan, add two tablespoons of powdered sugar and reduce the liquid by simmering over low heat. Set aside to cool.

MAKE THE BUTTERCREAM:

Step 1: Place butter on a kitchen countertop and leave it until it reaches room temperature.

Step 2: In a blender, puree blueberries and milk until smooth. Transfer into a small saucepan, add two tablespoons of powdered sugar and reduce the liquid by simmering over low heat. Set aside to cool.

Step 3: In a bowl of stand mixer, fitted with the paddle attachment, beat butter on medium speed, for 3-4 minutes until it becomes soft and light.

Step 4: Gradually add one half of powdered sugar and beat starting on low speed and continuing on medium speed until fully incorporated. Add vanilla extract and beat again for another 30 seconds.

Step 5: Add blueberries puree and beat on medium speed until fully incorporated.

Step 6: Add remaining powdered sugar and beat the mixture until smooth.

Place into the fridge to cool.

Store Blueberry Buttercream in the refrigerator for up to one week. Beat it with a mixer before using.

Dark Horse Chocolate Cream Cheese Buttercream

Amazing buttercream for chocolate cake.

INGREDIENTS:

16 Oz **Cream cheese**, softened

8 Oz **Butter**, unsalted, softened

2 cups **Sugar**, powdered

1/2 cup **Cocoa powder**, Dutch, unsweetened

1 teaspoon **Vanilla**, pure, extract

EQUIPMENT:

Stand or hand mixer fitted with the paddle attachment, Medium mixing bowl, Cake decorating piping tips and bags (optional).

PREPARATION:

Step 1: Place butter and cream cheese on a kitchen countertop and leave it until it reaches room temperature.

Step 2: In a medium mixing bowl combine powdered sugar and Dutch cocoa powder. Set aside.

Step 3: In a bowl of stand mixer, fitted with the paddle attachment, add cream cheese and beat it at a medium speed until mixture becomes smooth.

Little by little, add softened butter and continue mixing until it becomes smooth and fluffy.

Step 4: Add vanilla extract; gradually add powdered sugar and cocoa powder mix, constantly beating on medium speed until all is fully incorporated and buttercream becomes light and fluffy.

Place into the fridge to cool.

Store Dark Chocolate Cream Cheese Buttercream in the refrigerator for up to one week. Beat it with a mixer before using.

Almond Vanilla Icing

INGREDIENTS:

2 cups **Sugar**, powdered, sifted

2 ½ tablespoons **Cream**, light

1 teaspoon **Almond**, pure, extract

1 teaspoon **Vanilla**, pure, extract

¼ teaspoon **Salt**

EQUIPMENT:

Stand or hand mixer fitted with the paddle attachment, Food scale or measuring cups set, Sifter, Cake decorating piping tips and bags (optional).

PREPARATION:

Step 1: In a medium bowl, combine light cream, almond extract, vanilla extract, and salt. Whisk until combined.

Step 2: Little by little, add powdered sugar. Whisk to form a thick icing.

Place into the fridge to cool.

Store Almond Vanilla Buttercream in the refrigerator for up to one week. Beat it with a mixer before using.

Banana Buttercream

INGREDIENTS:

8 Oz **Butter**, unsalted, softened

2 cups **Sugar**, powdered, sifted

2 tablespoons **Milk,** whole

1 Banana, **ripe**

1 teaspoon **Vanilla**, pure, extract

EQUIPMENT:

Stand or hand mixer fitted with the paddle attachment, Food processor, Sifter, Food scale or measuring cups set, Cake decorating piping tips and bags (optional).

PREPARATION:

Step 1: Place butter on a kitchen countertop and leave it until it reaches room temperature.

Step 2: In a food processor, puree banana until creamy consistency. Set aside.

Step 3: In a bowl of stand mixer, fitted with the paddle attachment, beat butter on medium speed, for 3-4 minutes until it becomes soft and light.

Step 4: Gradually add one half of powdered sugar

and beat starting on low speed and continuing on medium speed until fully incorporated. Add vanilla extract and beat again for 30 seconds.

Step 5: Add banana puree and process until all is incorporated.

Step 6: Add remaining powdered sugar and process mixture until smooth. Do not overbeat.

Place into the fridge to cool.

Store Banana Buttercream in the refrigerator for up to one week. Beat it with a mixer before using.

Banana Cream Cheese Buttercream

INGREDIENTS:

8 Oz **Butter**, unsalted, softened

8 Oz **Cream cheese**, softened

2 cups **Sugar**, powdered, sifted

1 Banana, **ripe**

1 teaspoon **Vanilla**, pure, extract

EQUIPMENT:

Stand or hand mixer fitted with the paddle attachment, Sifter, Food processor, Food scale or measuring cups set, Cake decorating piping tips and bags (optional).

PREPARATION:

Step 1: Place butter and cream cheese on a kitchen countertop and leave it until it reaches room temperature.

Step 2: In a food processor, puree banana until creamy consistency. Set aside.

Step 3: In a bowl of stand mixer, fitted with the paddle attachment, beat cream cheese on medium speed, for 4-5 minutes until it achieved a smooth consistency.

Step 4: Add softened butter, (one quarter at a time) and beat on medium speed until mixture becomes soft and light.

Step 5: Gradually add one half of powdered sugar and beat, starting on low speed and continuing on medium speed, until fully incorporated. Add vanilla extract and beat for another 30 seconds.

Step 6: Add banana puree and process until all is incorporated.

Step 7: Add remaining powdered sugar and beat until all is incorporated and buttercream becomes smooth and fluffy.

Place into the fridge to cool.

Store Banana Cream Cheese Buttercream in the refrigerator for up to one week. Beat it with a mixer before using.

Banana Caramel Buttercream

INGREDIENTS:

4 Oz **Butter**, unsalted, softened

1 ½ cups **Sugar**, powdered, sifted

1 cup **Sugar**, brown

1 Banana, **ripe**

¼ cup **Heavy cream**

1 teaspoon **Vanilla**, pure, extract

¼ teaspoon **Salt**

EQUIPMENT:

Stand or hand mixer fitted with the paddle attachment, Medium size saucepan, Sifter, Food scale or measuring cups set, Cake decorating piping tips and bags (optional).

PREPARATION:

Step 1: In a food processor, puree banana until creamy consistency. Set aside.

Step 2: In a saucepan, melt butter over low heat. Add brown sugar and heavy cream.

Cook the mixture stirring, until the mixture starts

bubbling and smells like caramel.

Remove from heat, add vanilla extract, and salt. Let it cool for a few minutes.

Step 3: Transfer caramel into a bowl of stand mixer, add one-quarter of powdered sugar. Beat on low speed until all is incorporated, then increase speed to medium.

Add vanilla extract and salt. Beat for another 30 seconds.

Step 4: Add banana puree and process until all is incorporated.

Step 5: Little by little, keep adding the rest of powdered sugar and beat until all is incorporated and the mixture is smooth and light.

Place into the fridge to cool.

Store Banana Caramel Buttercream in the refrigerator for up to 1 week. Beat it with a mixer before using.

Strawberry Glaze

INGREDIENTS:

4 Oz **Strawberries**, fresh or frozen, thawed & drained

2 Oz **Butter**, unsalted, softened

2 cups **Sugar**, powdered, sifted

2 tablespoon **Milk,** whole

1 teaspoon **Vanilla**, pure, extract

¼ teaspoon **Salt**

EQUIPMENT:

Stand or hand mixer fitted with the paddle attachment, Medium size saucepan, Sifter, Food processor, Food scale or measuring cups set, Cake decorating piping tips and bags (optional).

PREPARATION:

Step 1: In a food processor, puree strawberries until creamy consistency. Set aside.

Step 2: In a saucepan, melt butter over low heat.

Remove from heat. Add powdered sugar, milk, vanilla extract, and salt. Let it cool for a few minutes.

Step 3: Remove from heat, add powdered sugar, milk, vanilla extract, and salt. Let it cool for a few minutes.

Step 4: Add creamed strawberries and process until all is incorporated and smooth.

Place into the fridge to cool.

Store Strawberry Glaze in the refrigerator for up to 1 week. Beat it with a mixer before using.

Unbaked Meringue Icing

This meringue is amazingly creamy and fluffy.

INGREDIENTS:

2 **Egg whites**

1/4 cup **Sugar**, powdered

1/4 cup **Maple syrup**

3 tablespoons **Water**

1/8 teaspoon **Cream of tartar**

1/4 teaspoon **Salt**

EQUIPMENT:

Stand or hand mixer fitted with the paddle attachment, Medium saucepan, Candy thermometer, Cake decorating piping tips and bags (optional).

PREPARATION:

Step 1: In a medium saucepan, combine sugar, maple syrup, water, cream of tartar, and salt. Cook on medium heat, stirring until mixture comes to a boil and sugar dissolves. Remove from heat. Cool to lukewarm (110°F).

Step 2: In a bowl of stand mixer fitted with the

paddle attachment add egg whites and beat on medium speed until foamy.

Slowly pour lukewarm syrup mixture. Beat on high speed until it forms stiff peaks.

If you desire brown meringue, place it into the oven to brown.

Place into the fridge to cool.

Store Unbaked Meringue Icing in the refrigerator for up to one week. Beat it with a mixer before using.

This recipe contains raw egg. We recommend that pregnant women, young children, the elderly, and the infirm do not consume raw egg.

Cinnamon Glaze

INGREDIENTS:

2 Oz **Butter**, unsalted, softened

2 cups **Sugar**, powdered, sifted

2 tablespoons **Cream,** heavy

1 tablespoon **Cinnamon,** powder

1 teaspoon **Vanilla**, pure, extract

¼ teaspoon **Salt**

EQUIPMENT:

Stand or hand mixer fitted with the paddle attachment, Medium size saucepan, Sifter, Food processor, Food scale or measuring cups set, Cake decorating piping tips and bags (optional).

PREPARATION:

Step 1: In a saucepan, melt butter over low heat.

Remove from heat, add powdered sugar, milk, vanilla extract, and salt. Let it cool for a few minutes.

Step 2: Transfer the mixture into a bowl of stand mixer. Beat on medium speed for 5 minutes, until smooth and creamy.

Step 3: Add cinnamon powder and process until all is incorporated and smooth.

Place into the fridge to cool.

Store Cinnamon Glaze in the refrigerator for up to one week. Beat it with a mixer before using.

Pineapple Coconut Buttercream

INGREDIENTS:

4 Oz **Butter**, unsalted, softened

4 cups **Sugar**, powdered, sifted

½ cup **Coconut**, shredded, unsweetened

1 tablespoon **Pineapples**, well drained, crushed

1 tablespoon **Pineapples**, juice of

1 teaspoon **Key Lime**, juice of

EQUIPMENT:

Stand or hand mixer fitted with the paddle attachment, Food processor, Sifter, Mesh sieve, Food scale or measuring cups set, Cake decorating piping tips and bags (optional).

PREPARATION:

Step 1: Place butter on a kitchen countertop and leave it until it reaches room temperature.

Step 2: In a food processor, process shredded coconut until it achieved a butter-like consistency.

Step 3: Separate juice from crushed pineapple into a small bowl. Set aside.

Step 4: In a bowl of stand mixer, fitted with the paddle attachment, beat butter on medium speed, for 3-4 minutes until it becomes soft and light.

Add coconut "butter" and beat on medium speed until all is incorporated.

Step 5: Gradually add one half of powdered sugar and beat starting on low speed and continuing on medium speed until fully incorporated. Add key lime juice and beat again for 30 seconds.

Step 6: Add crushed, drained pineapples and pineapple juice. Beat until all is incorporated.

Step 7: Add remaining powdered sugar and process buttercream until smooth.

Place into the fridge to cool.

Store Pineapple Coconut Buttercream in the refrigerator for up to one week. Beat it with a mixer before using.

Maple Meringue Icing

This meringue is amazingly creamy and fluffy.

INGREDIENTS:

6 **Egg whites**

2 cups **Sugar**, white, powdered

3 cups **Butter**, unsalted, melted

¼ cup Maple Syrup, pure

¼ teaspoon **Salt**

EQUIPMENT:

Stand or hand mixer fitted with the paddle attachment, Medium saucepan, Candy thermometer, Cake decorating piping tips and bags (optional).

PREPARATION:

Step 1: In a medium saucepan, combine sugar, maple syrup, water, cream of tartar, and salt. Cook over medium heat, stirring until mixture comes to a boil and sugar dissolves. Remove from heat. Cool to lukewarm (110°F).

Step 2: In a bowl of a stand mixer, fitted with a paddle attachment, beat egg whites on medium speed until foamy.

Slowly pour lukewarm syrup mixture. Beat on high speed until it forms stiff peaks.

If you desire brown meringue, place into the oven to brown.

Place into the fridge to cool.

Store Maple Meringue Icing in the refrigerator for up to 1 week. Beat it with a mixer before using.

This recipe contains raw egg. We recommend that pregnant women, young children, the elderly, and the infirm do not consume raw egg.

Marshmallow Buttercream

INGREDIENTS:

13 Oz **Marshmallow**, fluff

4 Oz **Strawberries,** fresh or frozen, thawed

2 cups **Butter**, unsalted, softened

2 ½ cups **Sugar**, powdered

1 teaspoon **Vanilla**, pure, extract

EQUIPMENT:

Stand or hand mixer fitted with the paddle attachment, Cake decorating piping tips and bags (optional).

PREPARATION:

Step 1: Place butter on a kitchen countertop and leave it until it reaches room temperature.

Step 2: In a bowl of stand mixer, fitted with the paddle attachment, beat butter on medium speed, for 3-4 minutes until it becomes soft and light.

Step 3: Gradually add powdered sugar and beat until fully incorporated. Add vanilla extract and beat again for 1-2 minutes.

Step 4: Drain thawed strawberries (if you are using

frozen). Add strawberries to the mixture and beat until all is combined.

Step 5: Fold in marshmallow fluff and mix to incorporate.

Place into the fridge to cool.

Store Marshmallow Buttercream in the refrigerator for up to one week. Beat it with a mixer before using.

Caramel Buttercream

INGREDIENTS:

1/3 cup **Butter**, unsalted, softened

2 ½ cups **Sugar**, cane, powdered

1 cup **Sugar**, brown

¼ cup **Cream,** heavy

1 teaspoon **Vanilla**, pure, extract

EQUIPMENT:

Stand or hand mixer fitted with the paddle attachment, Medium saucepan, Cake decorating piping tips and bags (optional).

PREPARATION:

Step 1: Melt butter over medium heat in a medium saucepan. Add brown sugar and bring it to boil. Reduce heat to low and simmer for another 2 minutes, stirring.

Add heavy cream and bring it to boil again, stirring. Remove from heat and set aside to cool. Add vanilla and mix until it is incorporated.

Step 2: Transfer the mixture into a bowl of stand

mixer, fitted with the paddle attachment. Add powdered sugar and beat until mixture becomes soft and smooth. Do not overbeat.

Store Caramel Buttercream in the refrigerator for up to one week. Beat it with a mixer before using.

Vegan Peanut Buttercream

INGREDIENTS:

1 cup **Peanut butter**

2 ½ cups **Sugar**, powdered

½ cups **Shortening,** vegetable

¼ cup **Milk,** coconut

1 teaspoon **Vanilla**, pure, extract

EQUIPMENT:

Stand or hand mixer fitted with the paddle attachment, Medium saucepan; Cake decorating piping tips and bags (optional).

PREPARATION:

Step 1: Place vegetable shortening on a kitchen countertop and leave it until it reaches room temperature.

Step 2: In a bowl of stand mixer, fitted with the paddle attachment, beat vegetable shortening on medium speed until it becomes soft. Add peanut butter and vanilla and beat on medium for 5-6 minutes.

Add powdered sugar and coconut milk. Beat low-medium speed until it becomes light and fluffy.

Store Vegan Peanut Buttercream in the refrigerator for up to one week. Beat it with a mixer before using.

White-Dark Chocolate Buttercream

INGREDIENTS:

2 cups **Cream**, heavy, whipping

8 Oz **Chocolate**, chips, dark

8 Oz **Chocolate**, chips, white

1 cup **Sugar**, powdered, sifted

2 teaspoons **Vanilla**, pure, extract

EQUIPMENT:

Stand or hand mixer fitted with the paddle attachment, Sifter, Small saucepan, Food scale or measuring cups set, Cake decorating piping tips and bags (optional).

PREPARATION:

Step 1: In a mixing bowl of a stand mixer combine dark and white chocolate chips.

Step 2: In a small saucepan, add heavy cream and bring it to boil. Remove from heat and pour over the chocolate chips, stirring, until chips melt. Set aside to cool for 4-5 minutes.

Add powdered sugar and beat on medium until mixture becomes smooth.

Refrigerate for at least 30 minutes until it cools down completely. Beat cooled mixture with a mixer before using until it becomes light and fluffy.

Store White-Dark Chocolate Buttercream in the refrigerator for up to one week. Beat it with a mixer before using.

Maple Buttercream

INGREDIENTS:

8 Oz **Butter**, unsalted, softened

2 cups **Sugar**, powdered, sifted

2 tablespoons **Milk,** whole

2 tablespoons **Maple syrup**, pure

2 teaspoons **Maple**, pure, extract

EQUIPMENT:

Stand or hand mixer fitted with the paddle attachment, Sifter, Food scale or measuring cups set, Cake decorating piping tips and bags (optional).

PREPARATION:

Step 1: Place butter on a kitchen countertop and leave it until it reaches room temperature.

Step 2: In a bowl of stand mixer, fitted with the paddle attachment, beat butter on medium speed, for 4-5 minutes until it becomes soft and light.

Step 3: Gradually add one half of powdered sugar and beat starting on low speed and continuing on medium speed until fully incorporated.

Add maple extract and maple syrup. Beat again for 1-2 minutes.

Slowly add remaining sugar and beat on medium speed until all is fully incorporated and buttercream becomes light and fluffy.

Place into the fridge to cool.

Store Maple Buttercream in the refrigerator for up to one week. Beat it with a mixer before using.

Chocolate Buttercream

INGREDIENTS:

8 Oz **Butter**, unsalted, softened

2 cups **Sugar**, powdered, sifted

½ cup **Cocoa powder,** Dutch, processed

2 tablespoons **Milk**

1 teaspoon **Vanilla**, pure, extract

EQUIPMENT:

Stand or hand mixer fitted with the paddle attachment, Sifter, Food scale or measuring cups set, Cake decorating piping tips and bags (optional).

PREPARATION:

Step 1: Place butter on a kitchen countertop and leave it until it reaches room temperature.

Step 2: In a bowl of stand mixer, fitted with the paddle attachment, beat butter on medium speed, for 3-4 minutes until it becomes soft and light.

Step 3: Gradually add one half of powdered sugar and beat starting on low speed and continuing on medium speed until fully incorporated.

Add vanilla extract and cocoa powder. Beat again for 30 seconds.

Slowly add remaining sugar and beat on medium speed until all is fully incorporated and buttercream becomes fluffy.

Place into the fridge to cool.

Store Chocolate Buttercream in the refrigerator for up to one week. Beat it with a mixer before using.

Cherry Buttercream

INGREDIENTS:

FOR THE BUTTERCREAM:

8 Oz **Butter**, unsalted, softened

2 cups **Sugar**, powdered, sifted

2 teaspoons **Vanilla**, pure, extract

FOR THE CHERRIES PUREE:

1 cup **Cherries**, frozen, thawed

2 tablespoons **Cream**, heavy, whipping

EQUIPMENT:

Stand or hand mixer fitted with the paddle attachment, Sifter, Food scale or measuring cups set, Cake decorating piping tips and bags (optional).

PREPARATION

MAKE THE PUREE:

Step 1: In a blender, puree cherries and heavy cream until smooth.

Transfer into a small saucepan, add two tablespoons of powdered sugar and reduce the liquid by simmering over low heat. Set aside to cool.

MAKE THE BUTTERCREAM:

Step 1: Place butter and frozen cherries on a kitchen countertop and leave it until it reaches room temperature.

Step 2: In a bowl of stand mixer, fitted with the paddle attachment, beat softened butter on medium speed, for 3-4 minutes until it becomes soft and light.

Step 3: Gradually add one half of powdered sugar and beat starting on low speed and continuing on medium speed until fully incorporated.

Add vanilla extract. Beat again for 30 seconds.

Slowly add remaining sugar and beat on medium speed until all is fully incorporated and buttercream becomes light and fluffy.

Step 4: Add cherry jelly and beat until all is incorporated.

Place into the fridge to cool.

Store Cherry Buttercream in the refrigerator for up to 1 week. Beat it with a mixer before using.

White Russian Buttercream

INGREDIENTS:

8 Oz **Butter**, unsalted, softened

2 cups **Sugar**, powdered, sifted

4 tablespoons **Kahlua,** liquor

2 tablespoons **Vodka**

2 teaspoons **Vanilla**, pure, extract

EQUIPMENT:

Stand or hand mixer fitted with the paddle attachment, Sifter, Food scale or measuring cups set, Cake decorating piping tips and bags (optional).

PREPARATION:

Step 1: Place butter on a kitchen countertop and leave it until it reaches room temperature.

Step 2: In a bowl of stand mixer, fitted with the paddle attachment, beat butter on medium speed, for 3-4 minutes until it becomes soft and light.

Step 3: Gradually add one half of powdered sugar and beat starting on low speed and continuing on medium speed until fully incorporated.

Add vanilla extract, vodka, and Kahlua liquor. Beat again for 30 seconds.

Slowly add remaining sugar and beat on medium speed until all is incorporated and buttercream becomes light and fluffy.

Place into the fridge to cool.

Store White Russian Buttercream in the refrigerator for up to one week. Beat it with a mixer before using.

Rum Raisin Cream Buttercream

INGREDIENTS:

FOR THE BUTTERCREAM:

8 Oz **Butter**, unsalted, softened

4 cups **Sugar**, powdered, sifted

½ cup **Heavy cream**

2 teaspoons **Vanilla**, pure, extract

2 tablespoons **Rum**

Pinch of **Salt**

FOR THE RUM RAISIN PUREE:

1 ½ cup **Raisins**, dried, brown

¼ cup **Heavy cream**

EQUIPMENT:

Stand or hand mixer fitted with the paddle attachment, Small saucepan, Sifter; Food scale or measuring cups set, Cake decorating piping tips and bags (optional).

PREPARATION:

MAKE THE PUREE:

Step 1: In a small saucepan, add raisins and heavy cream. Bring to boil and simmer for 4-5 minutes.

Transfer into a food processor and process the mixture until smooth and free of any lumps.

MAKE THE BUTTERCREAM:

Step 1: Place butter on a kitchen countertop and leave it until it reaches room temperature.

Step 2: In a bowl of stand mixer, fitted with the paddle attachment, beat butter on medium speed, for 3-4 minutes until it becomes soft and light. Set aside to cool.

Step 3: Gradually add one half of powdered sugar and beat starting on low speed and continuing on low-medium speed until fully incorporated.

Add vanilla extract. Beat again for 30 seconds.

Slowly add remaining sugar and beat on medium speed until all is fully incorporated and buttercream becomes light and fluffy. Do not overbeat.

Step 4: Add heavy cream and beat until it reaches

desired consistency. Do not overbeat or buttercream will clump.

Step 5: Add raisin mixture and rum. Mix again for 45 seconds until all is incorporated.

Place into the fridge to cool.

Store Ram Raisin Buttercream in the refrigerator for up to one week. Beat it with a mixer before using.

Red Wine Cream Buttercream

INGREDIENTS:

FOR THE BUTTERCREAM:

8 Oz **Butter**, unsalted, softened

4 cups **Sugar**, powdered, sifted

½ cup **Heavy cream**

2 teaspoons **Vanilla**, pure, extract

Pinch of **Salt**

FOR THE RED WINE SYRUP:

1 cup Wine, red

¼ cup Sugar, cane, powdered

EQUIPMENT:

Stand or hand mixer fitted with the paddle attachment, Small saucepan, Sifter, Food scale or measuring cups set, Cake decorating piping tips and bags (optional).

PREPARATION

MAKE THE SYRUP:

Step 1: In a small saucepan, add wine and powdered sugar. Bring to boil and simmer for 4-5 minutes or until the mixture thickens.

MAKE THE BUTTERCREAM:

Step 1: Place butter on a kitchen countertop and leave it until it reaches room temperature.

Step 2: In a bowl of stand mixer, fitted with the paddle attachment, beat butter on medium speed, for 3-4 minutes until it becomes soft and light. Set aside to cool.

Step 3: Gradually add one half of powdered sugar and beat starting on low speed and continuing on low-medium speed until fully incorporated.

Add vanilla extract. Beat again for 30 seconds.

Slowly add remaining sugar and beat on medium speed until all is fully incorporated and buttercream becomes light and fluffy. Do not overbeat.

Step 4: Add heavy cream and beat until it reaches desired consistency. Do not overbeat or buttercream will clump.

Step 5: Add wine syrup. Mix again for 45 seconds until all is incorporated.

Place into the fridge to cool.

Store Red Wine Cream Buttercream in the refrigerator

for up to one week. Beat it with a mixer before using.

Thank You for Purchasing This Book!

I create and test recipes for you. I hope you enjoyed these recipes.

Your review of this book helps me succeed & grow. If you enjoyed this book, please leave me a short (1-2 sentence) review on Amazon.

Thank you so much for reviewing this book!

Do you have any questions?
Email me at: **cookbooks@m-a-i-a.com and subscribe to our weekly free recipes. Please put "Recipes" in the subject.**

MARIA SOBININA
m-a-i-a.com & maiatea.com